# Helen Keller

### by Joanne Mattern

### Content Consultant
Nanci R. Vargus, Ed.D.
Professor Emeritus, University of Indianapolis

### Reading Consultant
Jeanne M. Clidas, Ph.D.
Reading Specialist

**Children's Press®**
An Imprint of Scholastic Inc.
New York Toronto London Auckland Sydney
Mexico City New Delhi Hong Kong
Danbury, Connecticut

Library of Congress Cataloging-in-Publication Data
Mattern, Joanne, 1963-
  Helen Keller/by Joanne Mattern; poem by Jodie Shepherd.
    pages cm. — (Rookie biographies)
  Includes bibliographical references index.
  Audience: Ages 3-6.
  ISBN 978-0-531-20593-8 (library binding)— 978-0-531-20995-0 (pbk.)
1. Keller, Helen, 1880-1968—Juvenile literature. 2. Deafblind women—United States—
Biography—Juvenile literature. 3. Deafblind people—United States—Biography—
Juvenile literature. 4. Sullivan, Annie, 1866-1936—Juvenile literature. I. Shepherd,
Jodie. II. Title.

HV1624.K4M37 2015
362.4'1092—dc23 [B]                                    2014035676

Produced by Spooky Cheetah Press
Poem by Jodie Shepherd
Design by Keith Plechaty

Printed in China 62

SCHOLASTIC, CHILDREN'S PRESS, ROOKIE BIOGRAPHIES®, and associated logos
are trademarks and/or registered trademarks of Scholastic Inc.

1 2 3 4 5 6 7 8 9 10 R 24 23 22 21 20 19 18 17 16 15

Photographs ©: Alamy Images: 20 (Courtesy CSU Archives/Everett Collection),
12 (Mary Evans Picture Library), 3 top left (Old Paper Studios), 30 top left (Pictorial
Press), 16 (Ron S Buskirk), 3 bottom (Tom Grundy); AP Images/USPS: 3 top right;
Corbis Images: 8, 15, 19, 28, 30 top right (Bettmann), 24; Dreamstime/Roman Milert:
31 center top; Getty Images/Imagno: 27, 31 top; New England Historic Genealogical
Society/www.AmericanAncestors.org: 11, 31 center bottom; Superstock, Inc./Library
of Congress: cover; The Granger Collection: 23, 31 bottom.

Map by XNR Productions, Inc.

# Table of Contents

# Meet Helen Keller

Helen Keller could not see, hear, or speak. When she was a little girl, she could not **communicate** with anyone. Then a special teacher helped Helen connect with the world. Helen went on to become one of the most admired people on Earth.

5

Helen was born on June 27, 1880, in Tuscumbia, Alabama. She was a normal and healthy baby.

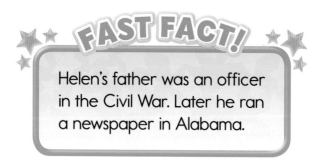

FAST FACT!

Helen's father was an officer in the Civil War. Later he ran a newspaper in Alabama.

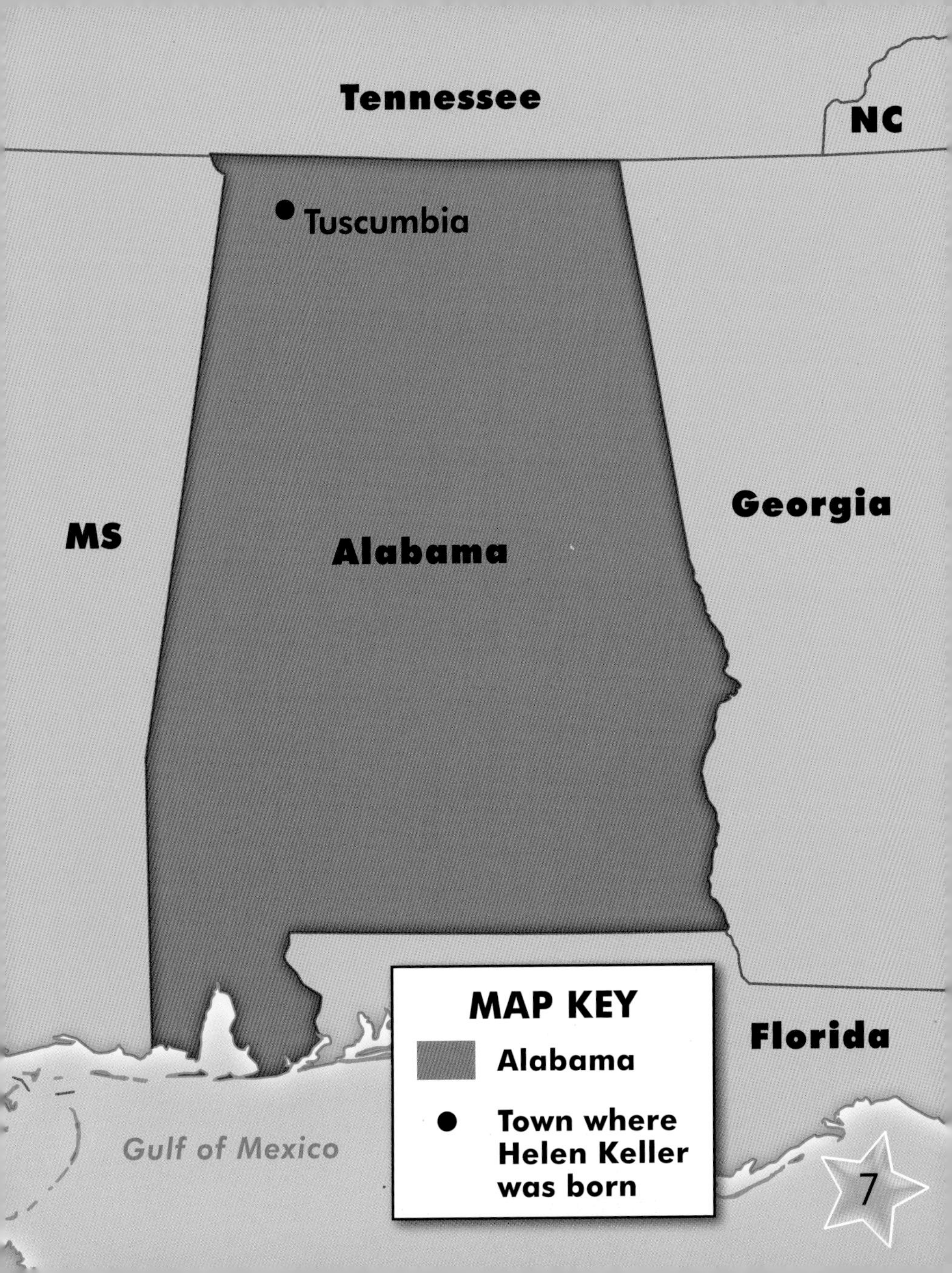

Tennessee

NC

• Tuscumbia

MS

Georgia

Alabama

Florida

**MAP KEY**

Alabama

• Town where
Helen Keller
was born

Gulf of Mexico

7

In 1882, little Helen got very sick. She had a very high fever. Her parents were afraid their daughter would die. They were happy when she got better. But the fever left Helen unable to see or hear. Because she could not hear, she also could not speak.

Helen is seven years old in this photo.

Helen was trapped in a silent, scary world. She became angry and wild. Her parents could not control her. They decided to hire someone to help. When Helen was seven years old, a teacher named Anne Sullivan came to live with the Kellers.

Helen (left) poses with Anne Sullivan.

Helen could not see the signs Sullivan made, so she had to feel them.

Sullivan taught Helen how to spell words with her fingers. The youngster learned quickly. But she did not know what the finger signs meant. Then one day, something amazing happened.

# "W-A-T-E-R-!"

Sullivan took Helen out to a water pump in the yard. She pumped water over the girl's hand. At the same time, Sullivan finger-spelled "water" into Helen's other hand. Suddenly, Helen understood!

A play was made about Helen's life. This is the scene when she learns what the sign for water means.

Helen's childhood home is now a museum.

Helen was very excited. She and Sullivan rushed around the house and yard. Helen wanted her teacher to spell the word for everything she touched. From that day on, Helen wanted to learn everything. It was the start of a new life.

# Helen's Education

Sullivan taught Helen how to finger-spell. She also learned how to read and type **Braille**. Braille is a special raised type that allows blind people to read. They can feel the special letters on the page.

Helen is reading a book that is printed in Braille.

Helen also learned how to read someone's lips by touching them as the person spoke. Later, Helen and Sullivan went to a special school in Boston so Keller could learn how to talk.

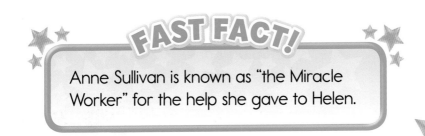

FAST FACT!

Anne Sullivan is known as "the Miracle Worker" for the help she gave to Helen.

Helen wanted to go to college. In 1900, she enrolled at Radcliffe College in Massachusetts. Sullivan went with her and helped her take notes. In 1904, Helen graduated from Radcliffe. She also wrote a book called *The Story of My Life*.

## FAST FACT!

Helen's **autobiography**, *The Story of My Life*, was made into a television special, a play, and a movie.

23

# Helen Meets the World

Helen became known around the world. Many famous people wanted to meet her. She met well-known authors such as Mark Twain. She also met many U.S. presidents and other world leaders.

An assistant helps Helen communicate with President John F. Kennedy.

25

Helen wanted to help other people. She asked the government to help people who were blind or deaf. She traveled around the world to show people how they could overcome their problems.

In this photo, Helen is reading to a group of blind children in Great Britain.

## Timeline of Helen Keller's Life

**1882**
loses her sight and hearing

**1880**
born on June 27

**1887**
begins working with Sullivan

Helen Keller died on June 1, 1968. She was 87 years old. Helen will always be remembered and admired as a woman who overcame huge obstacles to achieve her goals. Her amazing example continues to **inspire** others to change the world.

**1904**
graduates from Radcliffe College

**1968**
dies on June 1

**1924**
begins working to help the deaf and blind

# A Poem About Helen Keller

*She lived in a world that was quiet and dark,*

*and then came a teacher who lit a great spark.*

*Helen learned there's a word for everything in creation;*

*her love for life and learning became an inspiration.*

# You Can Make a Difference

- Work hard to overcome your challenges and help others who face their own.

- Look for creative ways to solve problems.

# Glossary

**autobiography** (AW-toh-bye-OG-ruh-fee): book a person writes about his or her life

**Braille** (BRAYL): system of writing for blind people that uses raised dots

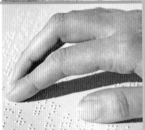

**communicate** (kuh-MYOO-nuh-kate): share information by speaking or writing

**inspire** (in-SPIRE): influence people to do great things

# Index

# Facts for Now

Visit this Scholastic Web site for more information on Helen Keller:
**www.factsfornow.scholastic.com**
Enter the keywords **Helen Keller**

# About the Author

Joanne Mattern has written more than 250 books for children. She especially likes writing biographies because she loves to learn about real people and the things they do. Joanne also enjoys writing about science, nature, and history. She grew up in New York State and still lives there with her husband, four children, and several pets.